WW
WOMAN OF WORTH

To

Jessica

Trust That this little book
will prove to be a blessing to you.

From

Grandma & Grandpa
Coughlan
with our love.

Becoming a Woman of Worth - Devotional

© 2007 Christian Art Gifts, RSA
Christian Art Gifts Inc., IL, USA

Designed by Christian Art Gifts

Printed in China

ISBN 978-1-86920-752-6

09 10 11 12 13 14 15 16 17 18 – 12 11 10 9 8 7 6 5 4 3

BECOMING A
WOMAN OF WORTH
Devotional

52 devotions on embracing
the woman God created you to be

Karen Moore

christian
art gifts®

CONTENTS

Introduction

*We encouraged you, and urged you
to live your lives in a way that God
would consider worthy. For He called you
into His Kingdom to share His glory.*
1 Thessalonians 2:12 NLT

How do you know if you're living a life that God would consider worthy? How do you discern His divine intention for your work, your home, your thoughts and your well-being?

In today's world, it's not always easy to hear, much less understand God's calling. If you've heard His voice and know He's called you, then He's already given you a special assignment. He's already helped you along the path of understanding so that you can discover what it means to Him to be a woman of worth.

Being someone God considers worthy

may not look quite the same as someone the world considers worthy. You may not be in a position of power, but you are at the throne of power at all times. You may not have the material possessions of the world, but you possess the wealth of the ages. You may not ever see your name in lights, but the Light of the World sees you.

Come on! Let's walk along together and encourage each other to become women that God would consider worthy. Let's examine His calling in our lives as we look at each letter that makes up the word "Worth" and define it according to His hope for each of us.

WORTH

You are meant to be a woman of
W-O-R-T-H. You were designed to
be closer to the heart and mind of
the Father. Let's begin by taking
our first "W", and define what it
means to walk closer with God.

Love not what you are,
but what you may become.
Miguel de Cervantes

Walking with Him

*If we live in the Spirit,
let us also walk in the Spirit.*

Galatians 5:25 NKJV

The writer of Galatians set a two-part course for those of us who desire to become a woman of worth. He suggested first that we must "live in the Spirit." What does that mean? Is it your intention to live in the Spirit today?

If you "live" anywhere it means that you are "alive" in that place. Perhaps the place where you come to life is at church. Maybe the place where you come to life is at home with your children and your husband. Maybe it's out there in the world where you do your job. It's good to know what makes you feel alive. It's good to understand just where you live.

If you live in the Spirit, you come alive any time an opportunity comes your way to share the gospel of your heart and mind. You come alive each time you whisper a prayer or lend a hand to your neighbor. You come alive with the love God has put in your heart.

As a woman of worth, you're alive in Him, and once you recognize that fact, there's no turning back. You're on the path and you're ready to walk. You're going to walk with His arm wrapped around you for the rest of your days. When you're walking in that kind of love, you're becoming an even stronger woman of worth.

A Worthy Thought

*We must not trust every word of others
or every feeling within ourselves,
but cautiously and patiently try the
matter, to see whether it is of God.*

Thomas à Kempis

Father in heaven, walk with me today
and help me to live in Your gentle and loving
Spirit. Guide me with each step to become
more of what You would have me be.
My joy rests in You. Amen.

Waiting for Him

The LORD is wonderfully good to those who wait for Him and seek Him. So it is good to wait quietly for salvation from the LORD.
Lamentations 3:25-26 NLT

Hurry to work; wait in traffic. Hurry to the bank before it closes; wait in line. Hurry to the doctor's office; wait to be called in. Hurry and wait. Hurry and wait. As women, we do a lot of that. Somehow gaining control over our time and our schedules is more difficult than we ever imagined. We're always in a hurry and we never like to wait.

How can we learn to wait? Even more, how can we learn to wait for God? We always like to think that His timing and ours will match up eventually. Often, it's true. Just as often, it's not. How can you wait in joy and in peace? How can you wait in holiness?

The Scripture says that it is "good to wait

quietly for the salvation of the Lord." What a great truth! Whenever we truly wait for the Lord, it is a matter of salvation. We're waiting to be saved from loneliness, or from illness, or from heartache. We're waiting to find the victory in life's drama and we're not sure our three little stones will be enough to knock over the Goliath we're facing. We're not sure, but we have hope. Why?

Because we know that the Lord is "wonderfully good" to those who wait for Him. He knows it's hard for us to wait. He knows we are finite. He knows and out of greater love for us than we could ever imagine, He waits for the perfect time to offer us salvation. He assures us that the wait is worthwhile.

A Worthy Thought

How wonderful it would be if our trust were so strong and our hope so victorious, that the waiting was simply an opportunity to prepare for the joy just ahead. Wait for Him. It's a worthy thing to do.

Lord, wait with me. Wait with me and strengthen my spirit in the certainty that You hold my life in Your hand and that You want only my good. Help me to wait in holiness and quiet joy. Amen.

A Woman of Wisdom

Let wisdom be your sister and
make common sense your closest friend.
Proverbs 7:4 CEV

Most of us think that we were born with common sense, or at least we hope we were. We do the things that seem reasonable and we treat others kindly and we think positive thoughts and do our best to make something good happen each morning when the sun rises once again. The truth is that we do have common sense most of the time. But, what God wants from us might be something different. God wants us to have "uncommon" sense.

When we're sisters with wisdom, we look beyond what others would say is reasonable. We move past the ordinary and we catch the fresh wind of everything extraordinary. We hold up our arms and reach out to the God of our hearts and minds and we embrace His "uncommon" goodness. We seek all that He would have us become because it is wise to do so. We are His family, His daughters, and His friends on this earth.

As a woman of worth, you often give the world the best of your wisdom, the mark of true common sense. As you do that, take one more step and walk past the thing that is expected and let the unexpected, the uncommon, the supreme goodness guide every action.

You were never meant to be ordinary. You were meant to do great things through the grace and power of the One who loves you. Embrace wisdom and let "uncommon" sense, the sense that everything is safe in your Father's hand, give you the hope you need for each day. Be a little bit regal today.

A Worthy Thought

Common sense is genius
dressed in working clothes.
Ralph Waldo Emerson

Father, help me to be wise in the ways that
matter. Help me to wisely put my trust in
You, embracing Your uncommon goodness,
Your truth, Your desire for me to live securely
and well. Let me walk in Your sanctuary
and gather the wisdom of the ages. Amen.

Such Beautiful Workmanship

*You made all the delicate, inner parts of
my body and knit me together in my
mother's womb. Thank You for making me so
wonderfully complex! Your workmanship
is marvelous – and how well I know it.*
Psalm 139:13-14 NLT

Do you ever forget just how wonderful you
are? Do you forget that you were beautifully
created and are the workmanship of a loving
Heavenly Father?

We live in a world that makes it pretty easy
for us to be hard on ourselves. We've got the
fashion industry dictating what we should
wear and the glamour magazines telling
us how to put it all together and the media
reminding us almost daily of the dismal failure
that comes from trying to be everything to
everyone. The world does not make you feel
beautiful.

Where can you go then to get a true reflection of yourself? Where can you find the right mirror to tell you that every curve, every angle, every tiny pore of your face and your body are artfully designed? That mirror is with you all the time and you can look into it any moment of the day.

You simply have to quiet your mind, bow your head, and take a peek inside to see the wonders that were artfully created within you. You are the reflection of your Creator and that makes you beautiful.

As you go about your day today, let the world keep its best and worst lists, its beauty standards, and its superficial identities. You have the real thing and it's part of what makes you a gorgeous woman of worth.

A Worthy Thought

Wonder is the basis of worship.
Thomas Carlyle

Lord, it is with awe and wonder that I embrace
the one that I am. Help me to shine my
light so others may know You. I am a woman
who is awed by the knowledge that it is
Your grace and Your workmanship that
have made me worthy. Amen.

Welcoming the Warrior Within

Without wavering, let us hold tightly to the hope we say we have, for God can be trusted to keep His promise. Think of ways to encourage one another to outbursts of love and good deeds.

Hebrews 10:23-24 NLT

Do you understand that as a woman of God, you are a warrior? You're the one who steps forth wearing His armor each day and riding with honor and persistence into the battlefields that are everywhere. It can even feel like you're walking in mine fields. It can feel like you have to watch every step because something could blow any minute.

Welcoming your role, growing as a woman of worth, you find yourself constantly thrown into the thick of things. It's a good thing you are so well prepared and so well armed. How do you prepare and arm yourself?

You do it by holding tightly to the hope you claim in God and trusting in His promises. You work diligently to encourage others to join in the battle, to stand up for all they believe and to put their hearts on the line. You plow through the front lines of the world, unafraid because you know the outcome and you know that what you're doing is making a difference.

As you read the Scriptures that fortify you and say the prayers that renew your spirit, consider your sisters in the field, warriors, who are with you in a great spirit of joy.

Spur each other on to even greater deeds and tender mercies. Be the first to forgive, the first to love, and the first to reach out with a willing hand. This is the armor that secures you in the ranks.

A Worthy Thought

Perseverance is the sister of patience,
the daughter of constancy, the friend of peace,
the cementer of friendships, the bond
of harmony and the bulwark of holiness.

Bernard of Clairvaux

As I turn my heart toward the work You
would have me do, Lord, remind me that
I am never in the battle alone. You are
always there, guiding and guarding and
showing me the way. Bless my sisters
everywhere who hold up the gauntlet of
Your love for all the world to see. Amen.

A Woman of Witness

You are like light for the whole world. A city built on top of a hill cannot be hidden, and no one would light a lamp and put it under a clay pot. A lamp is placed on a lampstand, where it can give light to everyone in the house. Make your light shine, so that others will see the good that you do and will praise your Father in heaven.
Matthew 5:14-16 CEV

Shine! You can't do otherwise when your heart is lit from within by the Light Source of the universe. Shine because you are meant to and shine because you must!

Women often labor under the illusion that they are supposed to keep their gifts and talents under a clay pot. They get confused about what it means to walk "humbly" with your God and what it means to shine your light. As in all things, it's a matter of heart and motivation. If your heart is bursting with joy that spills out no matter what you do, then keep on shining. If you're holding back because you're not sure it's okay to be a light in the world, then read Matthew 5:14-16 over again until it really sinks in.

You are a light, a woman of witness. You are the walking embodiment of the message God wants to bring to the whole world. He gave you His light so that others would see you clearly. He gave it to you so that you would never find yourself walking in the dark.

Put a plant in your clay pot and set it in the window. That way you'll both be in the light and offering your gifts of radiant beauty to the world.

A Worthy Thought

One loving soul sets another on fire.
Augustine of Hippo

Lord, help me to turn the light up this week.
Help me to understand that someone out
there is looking for You and that the only
way they might ever find You is through me.
Let me be Your light in the world. Amen.

A Woman Willing to Serve

My dear friends, stand firm and don't be shaken. Always keep busy working for the Lord. You know that everything you do for Him is worthwhile.
1 Corinthians 15:58 CEV

Women were born to service. Men were born to service. We were all born to serve each other because that is what God called us to do. What does it mean then to serve? Do we have to go out and find a soup kitchen or take a turn in the nursery at church? Well maybe, but let's look at what else it could mean to be willing to serve.

A willingness to serve as a woman of worth is all about attitude. When we serve others and inside ourselves we think something like, "I'm sure God is proud of me today. Look at all this good stuff I'm doing," we may be surprised to discover that we have employed the right actions, but we forgot to add the right heart. When we serve and congratulate ourselves for doing so, then we might have been "willing" to serve, but we're more interested in fulfilling an obligation or making sure others know we did our part.

The idea for us as women being willing to serve is that no matter what and no matter where and no matter for whom, we can only call it "serving" if we do it with the right spirit. If we're serving God, then everything we do must be done in love. If we're serving in love, we won't even stop to think about "how good we're being." Do you see the difference?

Serving each other in love is a full time, life time job. The interesting thing is that when we do all things in love, the act of serving becomes secondary. Let's always be willing to serve the Lord in every way possible.

A Worthy Thought

*You will find, as you look back upon your life,
that the moments that stand out are the
moments when you have done things for others.*

Henry Drummond

Dear Father, as I serve You this week, help me
to find strength through Your Spirit to offer
greater love to others. Help me to put the needs
of those around me first knowing full well that
as I attend to their well-being, You graciously
care for mine. Thank You, Lord. Amen.

A Woman of Worship

The earth is the LORD'S, and everything in it.
The world and all its people belong to Him.
For He laid the earth's foundation on
the seas and built it on the ocean depths.
Psalm 24: 1-2 NLT

Worship takes on many forms. Whether we're at church or at home or driving in the car, we can find a form for worship. Why? Because worship is a heart thing. It's about adoring, praising, loving and treasuring what we know and understand with the spirit. It's about giving God something back in a way that suggests we're in awe of all that has been done for us.

The psalmist reminds us that the "world and all its people belong to Him." That means that worship happens in every village, every city, every community around the globe where hearts are turned toward the Creator. Worship is not something we simply do, but it is a great part of who we are. We are beings that have been taught to love and to enjoy and to get excited about the gifts of life. We are part of a greater whole and it all belongs to God.

"The earth is the Lord's and everything in it." That statement is unequivocal. It does not give room for a second runner up. It is a truth and the more we embrace that truth, the more we can worship in real joy. We will feel it on the mountaintops and by the river's edge and we will feel it in the sanctuaries of our hearts and our churches.

We will be a walking form of worship every day that we begin to understand a little more fully that worship is a foundation stone of all that makes life real. A woman of worth worships with her whole heart and mind and soul.

A Worthy Thought

We should dedicate ourselves to becoming in this life the most perfect worshipers of God we can possibly be, as we hope to be through all eternity.

Brother Lawrence

Lord, let me dedicate myself to You and to worshiping You with the spirit of love and joy that come from a heart that is grateful for the many gifts You have given. Amen.

A Woman of Welcoming Words

Everyone enjoys a fitting reply; it is wonderful to say the right thing at the right time!

Proverbs 15:23 NLT

Words are important. What you say makes a difference. Take a moment and reflect on two things. Think about a time when someone said something to you that was entirely the wrong thing. Their words left you reeling from the impact of them. You were stung, disappointed and nearly blown away.

Now think about a time when someone said something to you that was equally amazing in its gift of kindness and love and the power it had to transform you, even if temporarily, so that life seemed better or more promising. Words are important.

Why is it so difficult to control the tongue?

Why do we glibly send out the slings and arrows of discontent, only to have them land on our own front doorstep? What we say comes from what we think and even when words are thoughtlessly spoken, somewhere inside we harbor the venom that brought the negative words to the surface. How do we stop the cycle of negative thought and unkind words?

We do it in part by examining our own motives. We search for understanding within ourselves about what triggers a negative reaction. If we find it, we can deal with it and become aware of it enough to be more considerate in future situations.

We know how good it feels to say the right thing at the right time. As a woman of worth, it's good to check your motivations. It's good to speak well of others.

A Worthy Thought

Words that do not give the light of
Christ increase the darkness.

Mother Teresa

Lord, remind me to be aware of my words.
Help me to be considerate of others and to
put their needs ahead of my own. Help me to
say the right thing at the right time. Amen.

The Gift of a Woman's Work

She is energetic and strong, a hard worker. She watches for bargains, her lights burn late into the night. Her hands are busy spinning thread, her fingers twisting fiber. She extends a helping hand to the poor and opens her arms to the needy.
Proverbs 31:17-20 NLT

Sometimes it's difficult for women to define their "work" because they are in a constant state of busyness. As the proverb relates, they are energetic and strong and hard workers. Regardless of whether or not you work outside your home, you're a busy woman constantly working for the good of those around you.

If, like the Proverbs woman, you're spinning your own thread, we applaud you. If not, you're no doubt spinning a number of projects into place as you spin through grocery stores finding the right balance of nutrition and bargains or spinning through the house tidying up after all those who seem to miss the socks on the floor or the dishes in the sink.

The value of your work is without measure to everyone. Someone, somewhere, is looking to you for help or encouragement or kindness. It seems likely that when God defines our work, He is looking beyond the things we do to create income, He's looking for the gifts that come to others through the Grace you share because of your faith.

He works through your hands, your intelligence, your kindness, your heart, and your desire to give. As a woman of worth, your work is a gift to everyone around you.

A Worthy Thought

Work with all your might, but never trust in your work. Pray with all your might for the blessing in God, but work at the same time with all diligence, with all patience, with all perseverance.

George Müller

Lord, bless the work of my hands that
I might do good things for You.
Bless the work of my heart that others
may desire to know more of You. Amen.

A Woman without Worry

"I tell you not to worry about your life. Don't worry about having something to eat, drink, or wear. Isn't life more than food or clothing?"
Matthew 6:25 CEV

Wouldn't it be wonderful to wake up each morning without a care in the world, with no worries whatsoever? If you truly understood how much you're worth to God, would it help you to worry less? I wonder!

The verse in Matthew that you have just read goes on to remind you that even the birds and the flowers are taken care of by God. Birds don't worry as they wing their way across the meadows. They know God will feed them. Flowers don't worry about being beautiful. They know they were born to be so.

The verse goes on to ask, "Can all your worries add a single moment to your life? Of course not." (Matthew 6:27).

If you really think about it then, if you really believe that in some way you're even more important to your Creator than birds and flowers, then what should you do with worry? Perhaps you should look worry right in the face and see what it is stealing from you.

Not only is it *not* adding a moment to your life, it is *stealing* precious moments from your life today. It is taking the moment you have now, that is perfectly beautiful, and trying to trick you into some "what if" thing about the future. You miss *now* and worry wins.

Practice living in moments of trust and joy and confidence that God loves you, cares for you, forgives you, and wants only your good. After all, God is good. He can desire nothing else for you. Each time you see a bird or a flower, remember your promise to yourself to live in the moment, free from worry.

Remember too, the promise from God, that He will clothe you, feed you, and take care of all your needs.

A Worthy Thought

Tomorrow has two handles: the handle
of fear and the handle of faith.
You can take hold of it by either handle.
Which one will you choose today?

Dear Lord, thank You for creating me as I am.
Thank You for the abundance I have enjoyed
since the day of my birth. I know I've had
abundance because I've lived in Your care
and Your love. Help me to hold on to Your
promises and leave worry behind. Amen.

Becoming
a Woman of Worth

You're becoming a woman of worth every day –
waiting and walking with love,
asking for wisdom, willing to serve –
worshiping God up above.
You're becoming a woman of worth every time
you witness with words of great care,
fighting for good from the warrior within,
working to give and to share.
You're becoming a woman of worth every day
and God loves you much more than you know,
blessing you, watching you, sharing the load –
rejoicing in seeing you grow.

W **O** R T H

Being a woman of W-**O**-R-T-H
means you're an original design.
You're open to God's leading
and obedient in serving Him.
Let's organize our thoughts around
this objective and see what it means
to offer God our constant and
continual open minds and hearts.
It's time to understand too what it
really means to be an Original,
to be what He created you to become.

You're an Original

*You saw me before I was born. Every day
of my life was recorded in Your book.
Every moment was laid out before a single
day had passed. How precious are Your
thoughts about me, O God! They are
innumerable! I can't even count them;
they outnumber the grains of sand!*

Psalm 139:16-18 NLT

No matter what the circumstances of your birth might have been, whether your parents planned for you or not, you're an original and God planned for you even before you were born. He knows all about you and as the psalmist tells us, He has so many precious thoughts about you, you can't even number them.

Imagine that! God's thoughts about you are beyond measure. He thinks you're totally precious. Can you grasp that? When your tiny fingers barely curled around those of your mother, He was bragging you up, knowing all that you would become and all that He knew you could be. You're an original! You're His design! There is absolutely no one, even if you have a twin, who is just like you. There is only *one* you and that means you're worth more than a human mind can comprehend to your Father in heaven.

As you wake to a new day or embrace a new week, thank God that you are exactly the person you are. Ask Him to guide your steps into becoming a woman of worth in the ways that He meant just for you. You're already a woman of worth in His heart.

A Worthy Thought

The greatest works are done by the ones.
The hundreds do not often do much –
the companies never; it is the units –
the single individuals, that are the
power and the might. Individual
efforts is, after all, the grand thing.

Charles H. Spurgeon

Dear Lord, I rejoice in knowing that You
know me so well. I thank You for
loving me, walking with me and
supporting my efforts in the world.
Help me to truly be an original servant,
a unique individual, growing, learning,
and sharing the gifts You've given me.
Amen.

Being an Orderly Woman

*This should be your ambition: to live a quiet life,
minding your own business and working with
your hands, just as we commanded you before.
As a result, people who are not Christians will
respect the way you live, and you will not need
to depend on others to meet your financial needs.*
1 Thessalonians 4:11-12 NLT

It's interesting to consider what it might mean
to be an "orderly" woman. It's also interesting
to imagine what being "orderly" has to do
with the things of God and becoming a woman
of worth.

If I look at my office space today, I might
wonder if I'll ever be an "orderly" woman
and yet I think this attribute may have more
to do with other things, such as ordering our
priorities and putting our lives in order.

When you approach life with a sense that
you desire to do all things in a patient and

orderly way, you're coming closer to becoming a true woman of worth.

These verses from first Thessalonians talk about living a quiet life and minding your own business. They talk about doing things with your hands, maybe arts and crafts, or sewing, or baking apple pies. It's a matter of living in a way that others will respect. More than that, it's about living in a way that others will desire. The benefit appears to be that all the things you need will be provided and you will never have to worry about your finances. Order then is an important thing to have in your life.

If your home is already in order and your desk is immaculate, you may not need to look at your physical environment to gauge how you're doing. Perhaps you need to see if your emotional life is in order. Living a "quiet life" is partly about living with hope and peace so that all is quiet within you and you can make the most out of any given day. Do a little inventory today and find out whether you need to put anything in your life in order.

A Worthy Thought

*First put yourself at peace, and then you
may better make others be at peace.
A peaceful and patient woman is of more
profit to herself and to others, too, than
a learned woman who has no peace.*

Adapted from Thomas à Kempis

Lord, help me choose to order my life in
such a way, that those observing me will
see Your peace and patience and not my
chaos and upheaval. Let me order my quiet
times so that my life experience will be one
of greater joy and peace today. Amen.

An Obedient Woman

Faithfully obey My laws, and I will send rain to make your crops grow and your trees produce fruit. Your harvest of grain and grapes will be so abundant, that you won't know what to do with it all. You will eat and be satisfied, and you will live in safety.

Leviticus 26:3-5 CEV

What is it that most of us crave more than anything else in this life? We want to know that we will be provided for and that we will be safe. We want to know that someone is watching and is taking care of our needs.

When God spoke with the early Hebrews about obeying His laws, He made them the promise that He would provide for them and not just by giving them barely enough to subsist, but by causing their harvest to be so plentiful that they would not know what to do with all the abundance.

You and I are rarely in the place of having so

much that we don't know what to do with it, but we are provided for and we are protected in our Father's care. When fear arises, perhaps we need to see where we have fallen short of the mark of obedience. Where did we slip up and allow that fear to come in? It can only enter if we give it the space to be there.

As an obedient woman of worth, you have the promise that you will be protected and provided for all the days of your life. You will eat and be satisfied; you will enjoy the harvest of God's gifts. When temptation comes, take a moment to discover what the consequences may be. If you step outside the bounds of the beautiful arms that hold you every day in protective care, you may find the price is too high to pay.

Check with your heart, it's your safety valve. Obedience then is about staying within the loving embrace of the One who cares more about you than anyone else ever could.

A Worthy Thought

It does not require great learning to be a Christian and be convinced of the truth of the Bible. It requires only an honest heart and a willingness to obey God.

Albert Barnes

Dear Lord, my heart desires to be in total obedience to Your will and purpose for my life. Help me to understand and to embrace all that it means to remain obedient to You in all that I do. Amen.

A Woman of Wonderful Opportunities

Honor Christ and let Him be the Lord of your life. Always be ready to give an answer when someone asks you about your hope. Give a kind and respectful answer and keep your conscience clear.
1 Peter 3:15-16 CEV

Wow! What a fabulous passage this is! We are blessed with opportunity beyond measure nearly every moment. What is the opportunity? It's the chance to bring hope into the life of someone else. As a woman of worth, your hope in Christ is crystal clear. It is evident in everything about you. It is there because you honor Him in all you do.

How do you do that? You do that by being ready to share your heart and mind and faith when someone asks for help, and sometimes even when they don't ask with words, but with deeds. You shine your light and with kindness and respect shed that light so that others can see your constant hope. The more you do this, the more God brings you joyful opportunities.

I have a sister who is always telling me that she wonders whether she does what God wants her to do. Mind you, she is a very faithful and prayerful woman and when adversity hits her life, she's continually on her knees.

After sharing thoughts about whether she needs to do more, she'll tell me stories of one person or another that she talked with at work and that she just gave them an example of how God's love works and the evident blessing that came from the things she shared. That's taking an opportunity and creating a God moment.

You share your story and His story and someone else wants to know more. That is the ministry of love. A woman of worth is a constant minister, embracing others, sharing kindness, honoring God. Let's all be sisters in that regard.

A Worthy Thought

If you're not lighting any candles,
don't complain about the dark.

Anonymous

Lord, open my eyes to opportunities to
share Your hope with others. Help me to
see when You have already opened the
door and someone is standing near me with
a candle that needs to be lit. Help me to
always carry a light and be ready. Amen.

A Woman of Positive Outlook

Let the Spirit change your way of thinking and make you into a new person.
Ephesians 4:23-24 CEV

*It's a beautiful world to see,
or it's dismal in every zone.
The thing it must be in its
gloom or its gleam
depends on yourself alone.*

Anonymous

Your attitude is everything. The reason the same three women can go to the same tea party and come home with a totally different view of the experience is largely a matter of attitude. One had a great time, one shared her heart, one thought the whole thing was stuffy! Whether you're feeling good about the sermon today or whether you walk away feeling like you didn't learn a thing, is also largely a matter of what your ears were ready to receive ... attitude.

A woman of worth is one who assigns a positive spin to the world and enlarges her perceptions to embrace those around her in a spirit of loving kindness. A woman of worth has changed her thinking, stepping outside of herself and her needs and her opinions, and opening her heart to all that is possible. Even when what is possible is off in the distance, she knows that her attitude makes a difference in how the journey feels. When you change your way of thinking, you become a new person.

Norman Vincent Peale reminded us to "change our thoughts and you change your world." Most of us don't examine why we think as we do or even if our responses to life have anything to do with thinking or not. Adopting attitudes of others is a worthwhile thing when you're living in a family or a culture that requires that, but even so, your personal experience in all of life invites you to review your thoughts and determine your course. If you've allowed the Spirit to help shape your thoughts and attitudes, you will see the world from a whole new viewpoint.

God's attitude toward us, in spite of us much of the time, is one of love. Can ours be any different toward each other? A woman of worth carries an attitude of love.

A Worthy Thought

Today I can murmur dejectedly because I have to do housework or I can feel honored because the Lord has provided shelter for my mind, body and soul. Today stretches ahead of me, waiting to be shaped. And here I am, the sculptor who gets to do the shaping. What today will be like is up to me. I get to choose what kind of day I will have!

Lord God, help me to choose to serve and view and live in the world today in a spirit of love, brought on by an attitude of joy for all that I have in You. Amen.

A Woman with an Open Hand and Heart

The generous prosper and are satisfied; those who refresh others will themselves be refreshed.
Proverbs 11:25 NLT

Most of us appreciate the delightful things we have accumulated over time. We have special treasures that bring us joy which we acquired while visiting a foreign land, or that we were given by our children or by a spouse on our anniversary. We're grateful that we have been so clearly blessed.

As we grow in our understanding of what it means to have possessions and what it means to give, we might see that God's Spirit offers us even more ways to look at those blessings. We can forever hold on to our special treasures and pull them out when a new visitor arrives and share them often. Or we may hide them away, hoping that no one will ever be able to take them from us. The challenge is to understand the difference between owning a possession or being possessed by it. Where your treasure is, your heart is, we've been told.

Whether we have large bank accounts or small ones, many possessions or few, the problem can be the same. Generosity is the requirement of the Spirit. When we are generous with others, it not only refreshes them, it refreshes us as well. The giving brings the joy.

Women are often open-hearted and generous. They volunteer their services, their skills, their time, and their love. Women of worth take one more step. They volunteer with a heart of total appreciation because they know that all they have is only borrowed. Their possessions are generous gifts of God. Gifts are meant to be shared. Make this a week that generously refreshes your life and your spirit.

A Worthy Thought

Who shuts his hand has lost his gold,
who opens it has it twice told.

George Herbert

Lord, You have been so very generous
with me. Let me be mindful today of
being generous in return with an open
hand and an open heart. Amen.

The Gentle Overseer

*When she speaks, her words are wise,
and kindness is the rule when she gives
instructions. She carefully watches all that
goes on in her household and does not have
to bear the consequences of laziness.*
Proverbs 31:26-27 NLT

Whether you work full-time from home, go to an office, or create a work environment in some way, you probably are still the primary overseer of your home. The role of homemaker is an honored position and one that has always been held in esteem from biblical times through today. The one who oversees a household does more than simply make sure the groceries are brought in and the meals are prepared.

You're the one who sets the tone for your home. The way you clean and cook and serve your family and the way you decorate and furnish and keep your home creates the atmosphere that all others come to know and respect. The old adage that a woman is the "heart" of the home is still very true today. As a woman of worth, you can rejoice in giving your heart and your kindness and your wisdom to all who enter your door.

An overseer of anything always has a choice. Whether you oversee an office of people, a basketball team, or your dinner table, you can choose to do so with kindness and respect, or in some other manner.

The Proverbs woman constantly chose kindness because that was the rule by which she did all things. Today's woman has the same choice. How will you oversee the things God has put into your hands?

A Worthy Thought

Care for the flock of God entrusted to you.
Watch over it willingly, not grudgingly – not
for what you will get out of it, but because
you are eager to serve God. Don't lord it over
the people assigned to your care, but lead
them by your good example. And when the
head Shepherd comes, your reward will be a
never-ending share in His glory and honor.
1 Peter 5:2-4 NLT

Lord, You've entrusted my family,
my friends, and sometimes even strangers
to my care. Help me be a blessing to all those
who share my home and my heart. Amen.

A Woman with Offspring

Train up a child in the way he should go,
and when he is old he will not depart from it.
Proverbs 22:6 NKJV

Children are a wonderful opportunity to keep learning. As a woman of worth, you're constantly learning and growing and becoming. You're ready to lead and share and plant dreams to help make the future secure and bright.

Whether you have your own children, or helped to raise your siblings, or help to raise children in your neighborhood, you know what it means and what it takes to "train up a child in the way he (or she) should go."

Jesus reminded the adults of His day that He wanted children to come to Him. He even said that the kingdom of God belonged to children. More than that, He said we must receive the kingdom of God as a little child would. What does that mean? How do you receive the kingdom of God in your own life?

Your childlike nature is an important part of who you are. Perhaps we are meant to never outgrow our innocent trust and delight in knowing God. Perhaps we're to receive the kingdom in this way every single day. If you've ever noticed how you feel when you have totally released your day to the Lord, over how you feel when the adult in you tries to control everything, you may have a glimpse of what we're after.

Consider this. Today, no matter how grown up you are, be the "offspring" of God and receive His Kingdom as a little child. Let the blessings flow!

A Worthy Thought

*Children are likely to live up to
what their fathers believe of them.*
Lady Bird Johnson

Dear Father, please help me to live up to what
You believe about me. Help me understand how
fully You love me and desire good for my life.
I receive You today as Your beloved child. Amen.

A Woman Growing Older

*Grow in the special favor and knowledge
of our Lord and Savior Jesus Christ.*
2 Peter 3:18 NLT

Most of us don't embrace the idea of growing
older. We've grown up in a culture that prizes
youth and energy and constant activity.

Now we're amidst a culture that refuses
to actually let us age because even at 50, we
can look 35, get a facelift, keep our hair dyed,
exercise every day and run a big company on
top of it all. Somewhere along the way, we've
lost the respect that once came with a bit of
God's frosting in our hair and a little less
flexibility to our torso.

If we are to grow in the special favor and
knowledge of the Lord, as Peter talks about
in the above verse, then we only have one
choice. We have to grow in every way. We

have to grow in mind, spirit, and body and understand the blessing that comes with the passing of time. We need to honor our graying hairs and thank God for the opportunities He has given us to grow and become more and change for the better. Few of us would want to return to our youth because we've worked too hard to get the knowledge about life and love and Spirit that we have today.

As a woman of worth, you are constantly growing. You are growing older and wiser and more beautiful with each passing day. You are rising in the special favor of God because you are becoming more and more like Him. Be grateful for each day and each moment that you are His light in the world. Keep shining way beyond your years!

A Worthy Thought

She is only advancing in life, whose heart is getting softer, her blood warmer, her brain quicker, and her spirit entering into living peace.

John Ruskin (adapted)

Lord, help me to rejoice in the years You've given me and add grace and peace and mercy to my days. Thank You for all I've learned and all I've lived to become more of the woman You want me to be. Amen.

Becoming
a Woman of Worth

You're becoming a woman of worth every day,
opening your heart and your mind,
growing in love as you kindly observe
your work and your family combined.
You're becoming a woman of worth every day,
obediently striving to share
the outstanding gifts you've been given,
and the offspring placed in your care
You're becoming a woman of worth every day,
with a positive outlook that knows
that the older you are, the more options you have
to be blessed with a spirit that grows.

R

W O R T H

Becoming a Woman of W-O-**R**-T-H refreshes your outlook every day, renews your spirit from within, and reminds you of all that God sees in you already. As you walk with Him, open your heart to Him and rejoice in Him, so you may become a more radiant, redeemed, and remarkable woman of worth.

A Woman of Reason

This is what the LORD says: Do not be afraid!
Don't be discouraged by this mighty army, for the
battle is not yours, but God's. Tomorrow, march
out against them. You will find them coming up
through the ascent of Ziz at the end of the valley
that opens into the wilderness of Jeruel. But you
will not even need to fight. Take your positions;
then stand still and watch the LORD's victory.
He is with you.
2 Chronicles 20:15-17 NLT

You may be wondering why I chose this
particular bit of wisdom from Scripture to share
in thinking about "reason."

I chose it because most of the time, as
women of worth, we are trying to make sense of
the world around us. We try to reason out what
happens, apply our faith to it and go on about
our business. Sometimes though, it becomes
overwhelming. Sometimes for no reason at all,
we find ourselves ill, or without a job, or with

family tragedies and nothing makes sense.

This section of second Chronicles reminds us of a number of things. One is that we simply do not have to be afraid. Even when the battle seems bigger than we could ever fight, we don't have to be discouraged. The battle is not ours, but God's. We may even be able to see the enemy coming up the hill, or camping around our home, or in our bank account, or the lives of our children, but we still have no reason to be afraid. We have only one thing to do. Fight? No. Take our position and stand still. Watch the Lord's victory.

How do you take your position? You put your reasoning mind, your worrying heart and your troubles in the one place where they can be safely dealt with. You take the position that God is fighting for you. You watch the victory that only He can bring as He is with you through every event and every challenge you might come across.

Don't be confounded by the enemy. Stand still and stand firm in your faith. God is with you and God loves you and that is reason enough!

A Worthy Thought

Reason is the greatest enemy faith has:
it never comes to the aid of spiritual things,
but–more frequently than not – struggles
against the divine Word, treating with
contempt all that emanates from God.

Martin Luther

Lord, help me to understand that reason
has its place, but You have an even
greater place, for with You all things
are possible. No matter how actively
enemies surround my door, remind me
ever that You are the sentinel. Amen.

A Woman of Responsibility

"Good people bring good things out of their hearts, but evil people bring evil things out of their hearts. I promise you that on the day of judgment, everyone will have to account for every careless word they have spoken. On that day they will be told that they are either innocent or guilty because of the things they have said."
Matthew 12:35-37 CEV

Women are responsible beings. God created us as people who are enormous care takers, responsible contributors to society, and leaders at home and in the community. According to Matthew, regardless of where we are or what we do, we are responsible for what we say.

You may get a bit of an uncomfortable twinge as I do, when I read the passage from Matthew about being accountable for every careless word you've ever spoken. That brings pause and it brings me to my knees. It brings me to the throne asking God to create in me a heart that longs to speak well of others, to others and to myself. What we say matters. God spoke the very universe into existence, "Let there be light." If what we say is creative energy, then we must realize the awesome responsibility of words.

A woman of worth speaks with responsibility. You must own what you say and be prepared to edit yourself at nearly every turn. The ego is strong and can even be an enemy to your spirit. Your ego wants the world to revolve around you. The Spirit wants the world to revolve around God. When your words come from a good heart, good things happen. Any other words need your commitment to seek forgiveness and change.

This is an area of responsibility that does not depend on your position or your finances or your geography. It simply comes from your heart. You can be the voice of love in a world starving for affection.

A Worthy Thought

Handle them carefully, for words
have more power than atom bombs.
Pearl Strachan

Dear Lord, I am so humbled by the awesome responsibility of words. Though it is my nature to strive to say right and good things to others, I know that I still struggle with this every day. Forgive my blindness and help me to serve Your truth in every word that comes from my lips. Amen.

A Woman of Respect

*Respect everyone and show special love for God's
people. Honor God and respect the Emperor.*
1 Peter 2:17 CEV

Most likely, from the time you were a little girl,
your parents and teachers aspired to have you
learn to honor and respect others. Sometimes
the idea of respect was coupled with fear. You
learned to respect a hot stove or a barking dog
and you learned to respect those in authority.
If you were fortunate, you especially learned
to respect your elders.

In the world today, respect seems almost
forgotten. Politicians badger each other, often
humiliating and disparaging each other for
our votes. Those in authority in our churches
abuse their powerful positions and cause us
to question why we believed in their roles
and their goodness. Parents disappoint

children and friends disappoint each other and husbands and wives hardly know where to start in communicating honor and respect to each other.

Even though the world may be bouncing around the planet, hardly respecting life itself, a woman of worth is called to a different view and a more desirable purpose. You are called to respect everyone and to show special love for God's people. You are called to honor God and even to respect the Emperor, who is the governing authority of the land. Imagine a world where we each respected the differences of others. Imagine honoring those you may disagree with. Imagine feeling that others honor and respect you.

What a difference respect can make. This is one arena where you don't have to wait for the world to "get it." You can simply practice it in every area of your life and watch beautiful things happen.

A Worthy Thought

Without respect, love cannot go far or rise high:
it is an angel with but one wing.
Alexandre Dumas

Lord God, I honor You in my life
and pray that You will help me
to honor all those I meet.
Even with those whose philosophies and
ideologies are not like mine, help
me to respect and honor their right
to believe as they do. Help me to
show Your love always. Amen.

A Righteous Woman

*Another reason for right living is that you
know how late it is; time is running out.
Wake up, for the coming of our salvation
is nearer now than when we first
believed. The night is almost gone;
the day of salvation will soon be here.*
Romans 13:11-12 NLT

Matthew Henry's father taught him the
following act of commitment.

*I take God the Father to be my God;
I take God the Son to be my Savior;
I take the Holy Ghost to be my Sanctifier;
I take the Word of God to be my rule;
I take the people of God to be my people;
And I hereby dedicate and yield my
whole self to the Lord: And I do this
deliberately, freely, and forever. Amen.*

As a woman of worth, you dedicate your whole self to freely love God, and to serve His Son and to embrace the Holy Spirit. You know that anything you do needs three-fold guidance to assure the outcome. You know it is your formula for right living.

We don't really think of ourselves as righteous these days, maybe because we worry so much about being self-righteous, which is nearly the opposite thing. To be really right before God though is a thing to strive for and we can get there, just as Matthew Henry suggests, by taking the Word of God and making it the rule. More than that, we can take the people of God and make them our people.

As the Scripture in Romans suggests, the time is upon us for right living. As you ask God to guide your understanding of what remains for you to become a stronger woman of worth, to live rightly before Him, remember that time is of the essence. He needs your warm and loving example today.

A Worthy Thought

*Let us have faith that right makes might;
and in that faith let us to the end dare
to do our duty as we understand it.*

Abraham Lincoln

Lord, for all the things in my life that are not
right, I ask forgiveness, and for those things
that You would look upon with favor,
I give You thanks. Amen.

Becoming Refreshed and Renewed

There must be a spiritual renewal of your thoughts and attitudes. You must display a new nature because you are a new person, created in God's likeness – righteous, holy, and true.
Ephesians 4:23-24 NLT

Most of you don't think of yourselves as Super Heroes, but when you look at what you take on and the pace of your lives, maybe you should. When you're carrying a full load, flying from one thing to another, it's hard to put the load down.

Sometimes, it can even feel impossible. The weight of that load then leads to other things that simply add to the burden ... not enough rest, too much coffee, too many fast food meals, too many nights of working an extra hour or two to get ready for the next day. When and how do you get a much needed break?

Put away the cape with the big red S that you probably embroidered yourself, and look inside yourself and be very, very still. When you accepted Christ into your life, your aim was to become more like Him and to have more of Him in your day-to-day tasks.

Maybe instead of Super Hero, that big red S should stand for Savior and you should give the cape to the one who really can take care of you. Jesus offered you the chance to give Him your burdens. Remember, He said, "Come to Me, all of you who are weary and carry heavy burdens, and I will give you rest" (Matthew 11:28).

This week, lay those burdens down and give yourself a chance to be renewed and refreshed in Him. Your real Hero is ready to help you.

A Worthy Thought

You have created us for yourself, and our heart
cannot be stilled until it finds rest in you.
Augustine of Hippo

Lord, be with me this week. Help me to give
up some of the weight that I carry, some of
the burdens of my heart and lay them at Your
feet. Help me to renew myself in You. Amen.

A Woman Willing to Take a Risk

I have observed something else in this world of ours. The fastest runner doesn't always win the race, and the strongest warrior doesn't always win the battle. The wise are often poor, and the skillful are not necessarily wealthy. And those who are educated don't always lead successful lives. It is all decided by chance, by being at the right place at the right time.

Ecclesiastes 9:11 NLT

You're a unique woman and you've defined yourself in a hundred different ways. You have your favorite outfits, recipes and dance steps, and you also have a touch of something else.

You've got a touch of renegade! You're totally comfortable with the idea that life takes a little risking now and then. You've proved it over and over. Chances are that every big thing you've ever done took a little extra risk to make it happen.

The teacher of Ecclesiastes may have been trying to send the message that life just happens. I don't really think that's the whole message though. We might read it as runners don't necessarily win if they don't get outside their comfort zone and compete just a bit ahead of their skill level. Warriors don't always win if they don't know how to pick their battles.

Being smart, or skilled or educated won't take care of things for you either. Maybe sometimes you have to step out and take a risk. When you do that, regardless of the outcome, you win. What would you risk for God this week?

A Worthy Thought

Be daring, be different, be impractical;
be anything that will assert integrity of purpose
and imaginative vision against the play-it
safers, the creatures of the commonplace,
the slaves of the ordinary.

Cecil Beaton

Lord, nothing about me is more special
than the next person I meet. Yes, You've
given me my own set of gifts, but I know
that I can either use those gifts in a very
comfortable way, or I can take a little
more risk and grow more like You. Help
me to be brave in all that I do. Amen.

A Woman of Relationships

We are all parts of His one body, and each of us has different work to do. And since we are all one body in Christ, we belong to each other, and each of us needs all the others.
Romans 12:5 NLT

I don't know about you, but there's almost nothing more wonderful in my life than my really close girlfriends. These are the friends who know all about me and still love me. They forgive me, they applaud me, and they stand beside me no matter what life brings.

As a member of the body of Christ, you're thrown into the world with a lot of different personalities. Some of them are soul sisters from the moment you recognize yourself in them. Some of them make you dizzy trying to figure out just what your role is all about in their lives. Some of them make you want to run the other way.

God made women especially good at relationship. We're His ambassadors in all the ways that bring peace and forgiveness and joy into a situation. We're His good deed doers and His hand-holding care givers. When it comes to relationships, He really counts on us to be His hands and His heart.

As it says in Romans, "we belong to each other, and each of us needs all the others." Whatever relationship you have with the women in your life, you need each other. Together you can teach each other to become more of what God designed each of you individually to be. Now that's a worthy pursuit, indeed.

A Worthy Thought

It's what each of us sows, and how,
that gives to us character and prestige.
Seeds of kindness, goodwill, and human
understanding, planted in fertile soil,
spring up into deathless friendships, big deeds
of worth, and a memory that will not soon
fade out. We are all sowers of seeds –
and let us never forget it!
George Matthew Adams

Lord, You have blessed my life with warm
and wonderful friends. Please help me
always to be a kind and loving friend
to each of them in return. Amen.

A Woman of Radiance

But let us who live in the light think clearly,
protected by the body armor of faith
and love, and wearing as our
helmet the confidence of our salvation.
1 Thessalonians 5:8 NLT

I'd venture to say that most of us probably consider our defense mechanisms to be more like literal body armor than like the concepts of faith and love. Our body armor is about protecting ourselves from the slings and arrows of life and the little whacks that have almost no meaning, but assail our spirits just the same. In our best defensive posture, we step outside, ready to take on the world.

Maybe we've been putting on the wrong armor. Instead of adopting one more defense mechanism, put on love. Wrap yourself in the armor of faith and you'll be protected from head to toe. In fact, make it a challenge to yourself this week to simply go about your business totally immersed in faith and love and see if you even need that defensive armor at all. Your invisible protection is powerful. The more clearly you recognize its presence, the stronger it is and the more you'll radiate the truth and the light to everyone around you.

If you were meant to shine, how can you do so if your armor is designed to keep the world at a distance? The armor of faith and love is not heavy and foreboding. It does not wrap up in itself and try to force its way around the neighborhood. It embraces each day, knowing that nothing can take away the perfect shine of faith.

So put a rose in the helmet of salvation and know with perfect confidence that you are loved and protected. You'll be a beautiful example of God's radiance.

A Worthy Thought

*As we let our light shine, we unconsciously give
other people the permission to do the same.*
Nelson Mandela

Dear Father, I know that I often walk around
with my defense mechanisms so poised to
fight that the light goes right out of my day.
Help me wear the armor of Your love
for all the world to see. Amen.

A Woman of Worth Rejoices

But let all who take refuge in You rejoice,
let them sing joyful praises forever. Protect them,
so all who love Your name may be filled
with joy. For You bless the godly, O LORD,
surrounding them with Your shield of love.
Psalm 5:11-12 NLT

Do you ever think about what makes you feel happy? When you are happy, do you behave differently than you do at other times, say when you're just too busy to think about it, or you're feeling a bit out of sorts with the world?

This week, think about those things that really make you happy. Make a list. Remind yourself of all the blessings you have. If you can't remember, visit a homeless shelter or do some public service, and your blessings will become abundantly clear.

Jesus said He came so that we could have

life in abundance, but probably few of us understand what He meant. Those who "get it" realize that we have absolutely everything. We have the keys to salvation. If you are still struggling with the idea of abundance, you may be expecting the wrong thing. Without being conscious of it, we focus on what we don't have. When we focus on the things we lack, we see ourselves as being deprived and by extension we assume that God is not paying attention to the details of our lives.

A woman of worth knows that rejoicing in God's love and praising Him for all that she has only opens the doors and windows to more light and more love and more possibility. Praise unleashes the power of abundance.

A grateful heart wins the day. Look at your vast fortunes and give thanks for everything. Chances are you'll run out of paper before you can begin to list the praiseworthy things that are part of your life today. Did I hear a hallelujah out there?

A Worthy Thought

If I was a nightingale, I would sing like a nightingale; if a swan, like a swan. But since I am a rational creature my role is to praise God.

Epictetus

Lord, I am truly in awe of all that I have received through Your goodness and grace. I rejoice in You and praise You for these abundant gifts of love. Amen.

A Woman of Worth Is Remarkable

A good reputation and respect are worth much more than silver and gold. The rich and the poor are all created by the LORD.
Proverbs 22:1-2 CEV

Do you have any female friends that you always think of as remarkable? Perhaps your friends say that about you! A woman of worth is remarkable in many ways. She knows the absolute value of respect and gives and receives respect from everyone around her. How does she do that?

When you have respect for another person, it means that you honor who they are and in honoring them, see the light of God within them. You protect their dreams and their plans and you offer a helping hand whenever you can. If necessary, you guard their reputation and recognize their value.

A woman of worth recognizes her own value as well because she knows that by the grace of God she is who she is and His thumbprint on her life makes her unique and yes, remarkable!

The Scripture says that respect and being well thought of are worth more than silver or gold. Anyone can have money, but not just anyone gains respect. In the world's terms, money is often the measure by which we assess matters of respect. If a person has a lot of money, we assume they are worthy of respect. If they are poor, we assume that they have not made good choices in life and so perhaps they are not worthy of our respect.

God made them all. As a woman of worth, when you see the light of God shining forth from someone you meet, you know they are worthy of honor and respect. God has chosen them to be remarkable! He's chosen you to be remarkable too.

A Worthy Thought

Success without honor is an unseasoned dish;
it will satisfy your hunger, but it won't taste good.

Joe Paterno

Lord, we sometimes lose sight of the fact
that with Your light, we are truly remarkable.
We are worthy because You have given
Your Son to make us so.
Thank You for Your ever-present love. Amen.

Becoming a Woman of Worth

You're becoming a woman of worth every day,
renewed by God's love and His grace,
refreshed in His care, willing to share
your kindness and loving embrace.
You're becoming a woman of worth every day,
respected for all you pursue,
reaching out with your heart, ready to start
a friendship with somebody new.
You're becoming a woman of worth every day
by shining your radiant light,
rejoicing each season for the remarkable reason
that you're totally loved in God's sight.

T

WORTH

It takes a lot of discipline to become a Woman of W-O-R-**T**-H and God is pleased when you try so hard to follow in His steps. He is your teacher and guide and requires only that you trust Him and treasure your time with Him. Be thankful for all that He shares with you to make your journey truly remarkable. You are His beloved child, no matter how many candles appear on your birthday cake.

Becoming a True-Hearted Woman

"Your eye is a lamp for your body.
A pure eye lets sunshine into your soul."
Matthew 6:22 NLT

As a woman of worth, you seek continually to have a true heart. You have a great desire to serve God and your family and those you care about with integrity. You want to reflect the sunshine that radiates from your soul.

It's not an easy thing to achieve and it takes a great deal of humility to even walk in that direction.

Fénelon said, "There is no true and constant gentleness without humility. While we are so fond of ourselves, we are easily offended with others. Let us be persuaded that nothing is due to us, and then nothing will disturb us. Let us often think of our own infirmities, and we will become indulgent towards those of others."

Everyone you meet deserves to see your light. All are in need of it. Wherever you find yourself this week, check with your heart to see if you are offering that light in truth, honoring your Father in heaven for all that He has done. If you find that you've been selective about your offering, then turn up your lamp. If you do that, they will see more of the true, loving God and less of the infirm and still striving You.

You've been called to be the light. As a woman with a remarkable heart, His truth will shine like the sun from you. Now doesn't that warm your spirit?

A Worthy Thought

*Everybody thinks of changing humanity
and nobody thinks of changing himself.*
Leo Tolstoy

Lord, turn up your light and let me shine
forth in the darkness. As I seek to
become a woman of worth, changing
my thoughts and my actions, let others
seek me to know more of You. Amen.

A Woman of Truth in Word and Deed

"When the Spirit of truth comes, He will guide you into all truth. He will not be presenting His own ideas; He will be telling you what He has heard. He will tell you about the future."
John 16:13 NLT

Most of us are geared more toward tomorrow than we are toward today. We don't realize how much time we spend planning and thinking and preparing for the future, and all the while, we are missing the present. The Spirit of Truth works in the present. He's the gift you have now for this very moment.

A woman of worth strives to hear His voice and receive His guidance in all that she does. She strives to be the embodiment of truth. It's been said that, "if you don't learn and know your truths, you cannot speak them. If you don't speak them, you will know a prison within. Tell your truths to yourself, and then to the others. The truth really will set you free!"

You must speak your truth and share your heart as God has given you strength and opportunity to do so. You are His voice and His hands and His heart and sharing that truth will add beauty and freedom to the present.

It's your day to listen, to walk and to share your blessings with those around you. Do it with grace and with a smile. If the truth sets your heart free, then all that you do will produce joy.

A Worthy Thought

*Let us begin by committing ourselves
to the truth – to see it like it is, and tell
it like it is – to find the truth, to speak
the truth, and to live the truth.*

Richard M. Nixon

Lord, it's not always easy to recognize the
truth. Help me to listen for Your voice and
the guidance of Your Spirit so that I might
live and speak and walk freely in You. Amen.

As a Woman Thinks

*This is what the LORD says to the people
of Israel: Is that what you are saying?
Yes, I know it is, for I know every
thought that comes into your minds.*
Ezekiel 11:5 NLT

Whew! I don't know about you, but I find this particular verse a little disturbing. Sometimes, without even getting an invitation, the weirdest thoughts will run through my mind, and I'll be grateful that no one actually has to know they ever showed up. No one, I guess, but God!

We may not be able to control every way-ward and good and ambitious thought that enters our heads, but we can make sure we think about what we're thinking about. In fact, that's an important thing to do. Like everything else, you have to discipline your mind with proper exercises and nourishment.

A healthy mind has to be trained.

A woman of worth understands the power of her thoughts and knows that the things she meditates on are the things that come into fruition. In this way, we literally help create our circumstances. If you've ever known someone who had a really negative life experience, chances are their thoughts were also negative. It's all about perception and attitude and about training your mind to think positively.

Discipline your mind with prayer and meditation and regular reading of the Word. Exercise your heart by giving and sharing from the light within. Nourish yourself with positive thoughts and keep in mind that we often are exactly what we think we are.

A Worthy Thought

*All truly wise thoughts have been thought
already thousands of times; but to
make them truly ours, we must think
them over again honestly, till they take
root in our personal experience.*

Goethe

Lord, you know everything about me.
Bless my thoughts and help me to discipline
my mind by paying constant attention to
Your thoughts and Your ways so that I may
become more worthy in Your sight. Amen.

A Woman
of Worth Is a Teacher

*God's servants must be kind to everyone,
and they must be good teachers and very patient.*
2 Timothy 2:24 CEV

Martin Luther said, "We must know how to teach God's Word aright, discerningly."

Those of us who influence others, and that's every one of us, know that there are many avenues for influencing the thoughts and actions of others.

As good teachers, we try a variety of techniques, but which ones work? The ones that work are the ones that fit the needs of the students. We're not trying to influence so others will think just like we do because we know what's good for them, although that is a tempting idea. We're teaching because God loves every person every bit as much as He loves us and wants us to find patient and loving ways to be a guide.

You're a teacher every day, regardless of your occupation. You teach others to have a positive attitude when you point out the sunshine instead of the clouds. You teach others to be reverent when you thank God for the gifts of joy and nourishment that you have in your life. You teach others to be humble when you step aside from ego and offer them strength in any time of need. You're a teacher and it is God's gift to you because it helps you to grow in His abundance. As Albert Einstein so aptly put it, "Love is a better teacher than duty."

As a woman of worth, your love is the gift you offer and each one who receives it learns something beautiful about walking in the light.

Be a patience teacher and a patient learner as well.

A Worthy Thought

Our critical day is not the very day of our death, but the whole course of our life; I thank them that pray for me when my bell tolls; but I thank them much more, that catechize me, or preach to me, or instruct me how to live.

John Donne

Lord, I am a willing student and thank
You for those who come into my life
and share their insights so well. I thank
You too for those who give me the
opportunity to share my understanding;
those insights so patiently taught to
me by Your Holy Spirit. Amen.

A Woman of Worth Is Tempted

No temptation has seized you except what is common to man. And God is faithful; He will not let you be tempted beyond what you can bear. But when you are tempted, He will also provide a way out so that you can stand up under it.

1 Corinthians 10:13

If we're honest about it, we know that we face the tentacles of temptation every day. We may only face it in small ways, buying new shoes when we just didn't really need another red pair, or having a little Godiva chocolate when we just prayed for help with a diet.

We're constantly assaulted with tempting things. Temptations can even seem like innocent distractions, but I wonder. How many times have you actually started out to tighten your budget, and in the same week, found yourself facing more reasons to spend money than you can count? How many times have you made a promise to yourself and to God that you would not let a negative word come out of your mouth, only to find yourself just a few moments later, saying something to a friend that you find appalling?

What's the answer then? Are we just slaves of temptation? Well, maybe. However, first Corinthians says that even though temptation is common, it doesn't have to defeat you. In fact, God already has a plan to help you out of it. Of course, the Tempter doesn't want you to know there's a way out, so this is a bit annoying to him.

Test yourself on this one. Make a little chart this week and note any time temptation has knocked on your door. Then give yourself points for how you answered. If you answered the door right away, you get 0 points. If you started to cave in, but finally walked away, you get 5 points. If you simply said, "I hear you knocking, but you can't come in," you get 10 points. The point is you can slam the door on temptation with God's help. Take a look at your scorecard and see who's winning!

A Worthy Thought

Temptation usually comes through a door
that has deliberately been left open.

Anonymous

Lord, I know I wouldn't get too many
points for my willingness to close
the door on temptation, but You
taught me a long time ago to pray for
deliverance from it, so I ask You once
again, "deliver me from temptation."
Amen.

The Thankful Woman

Always be joyful and never stop praying.
Whatever happens, keep thanking God because of
Jesus Christ. This is what God wants you to do.
1 Thessalonians 5:16-18 CEV

You know that attitude is everything and yet that gratitude attitude is not always easy to achieve. Sometimes you wonder if you'd even be somewhat crazy to think that way.

When you chose to follow Jesus, your club membership came with a clause that said something like, "now you have no excuses because you just became the child of a King and you have all things because of Jesus." Okay, maybe you didn't see that in the fine print, but the Scripture seems to confirm that your attitude should be easily read as one of total thankfulness.

The truth is that you've already got the abundant life. You've already got the best gift this planet ever had to offer. You've got it all because you're one loved and saved woman! You have a place to take your prayers and your heartaches. You have a shoulder to cry on and an arm to reach for when you simply need a hug. You have the listening ear and the endless forgiving love of the Savior.

Is your light starting to shine a bit more? Are you starting to see why you really can be always joyful even when the circumstances around you aren't exactly cheering you on or giving you a standing ovation?

What makes the difference? You! You make the difference every time you remember to say thanks for those little things that keep you going in a day. When you pause to bless the flowers or your cat or your friends, you see it. When you pray for those less fortunate than yourself, you see it. When you keep trying in spite of anything reason would suggest, you see it. You see that you have every reason to be thankful. Bring the light of Christ to life with every prayer!

A Worthy Thought

Thanksgiving is a good thing;
thanksliving is better!
Anonymous

Lord, with a grateful heart, I thank You for
all You've given me, especially in sharing
Your divine Spirit so that I can see
Your hand in all I do. Amen.

The Talented Woman

"You are the light of the world – like a city on a mountain, glowing in the night for all to see. Don't hide your light under a basket! Instead, put it on a stand and let it shine for all."
Matthew 5:14-15 NLT

Not feeling quite like the light of the world this week? Can't remember the last time you thought you could glow in the dark? Hold up your candle!

If your light is flickering a bit, maybe you just need the flame adjusted. As a woman of a variety of remarkable talents, you may have come to the conclusion that your special gifts are just something you were born with and not intended to make the world glow.

Think about the women you most admire. What is it that captures your attention about them? It may be that they have a knack for putting together the best church dinners you've ever attended, or that they can say a prayer that brings tears to your eyes every time. It may be that they simply offer you themselves every time they are in your presence. They never withhold their light. They are always willing, no matter how unwittingly, to simply shine.

A beacon can't really judge the intensity of its light. It does what it was designed to do. It shines forth in the darkness and guides those who are anywhere in the midst of its beam to draw closer. That's what you do with your talents no matter what they are. That's what you do with your light. You bring those around you a little closer to the Source that will keep them safe through the darkness.

If your light is somewhat hidden beneath the baskets of self-doubt and uncertainty that you have tucked it under, then bring it out, let it stand up with love and humility and shine for all.

A Worthy Thought

Use your gifts faithfully, and they shall be enlarged; practice what you know, and you shall attain to higher knowledge.

Matthew Arnold

Lord, whatever talents I possess came from Your love and Your guidance. Let me always share those in the best possible light. Amen.

A Woman of Tender Talk

Plans go wrong for lack of advice;
many counselors bring success. Everyone
enjoys a fitting reply; it is wonderful
to say the right thing at the right time!
Proverbs 15:22-23 NLT

Women are often characterized as being chatty. That would probably be a polite term. The fact is that most women are quite capable talkers and are willing to share their thoughts and feelings with others they care about. It's one of the wonderful attributes of women and I'm pretty sure God designed us this way.

The two proverbs above speak to very different aspects of talking, but both of them can be tender if we choose. When we're giving advice, we're not often certain what attitude we should adopt. Are we to be authoritative, motherly, friendly, or judgmental? It all depends on the desired outcome. If we're hoping the person will succeed in their plans, we might adopt one way of delivering a message. If we don't want them to succeed because we don't think the choice is wise or it doesn't match our opinion of things, we might deliver our message another way. Proverbs say that whatever our plans, things would go better if we seek advice from a number of sources, so we can make the best choices. Women of worth are valuable advice givers because they seek the highest good of the person they are talking to.

The second proverb deals with being able to say the right thing at the right time. Most of us would agree that we certainly aspire to that, but aren't always certain how to achieve it. We want to give a response to someone that makes them feel good. Our goal then is to talk tenderly, to give others our best thoughts and our most generous responses. When we do that, we're serving as God's ambassador of good will.

A Worthy Thought

Suit the action to the word,
the word to the action.
William Shakespeare

Lord, it's always important to me to say the right thing. Please bless any opportunities I might have this week to offer sound advice or kind words to those around me. Amen.

A Tough Woman

*The steps of the godly are directed by
the* LORD. *He delights in every detail of
their lives. Though they stumble, they will
not fall, for the* LORD *holds them by the hand.*
Psalm 37:23 24 NLT

Women today, as in each generation before
us, have had to exhibit immeasurable ability
to stay strong to survive. Our life experiences
are an amazing mix of beauty and tragedy and
there's only one thing we can do. We must be
tough and find our strength in the help only
God can give.

Jane Truax offers us this thought, "Botanists
say that trees need the powerful March winds
to flex their trunks and main branches, so that
the sap is drawn up to nourish the budding
leaves. Perhaps we need the gales of life in
the same way, though we dislike enduring
them. A blustery period in our fortunes is

often the prelude to a new spring of life and health, success and happiness, when we keep steadfast faith and look to the good in spite of appearances."

The Scripture tells us that God is aware of the details of our lives. He sees our needs and holds us by the hand. When we face the blustery trials, the gales of life, then we need to keep our grasp ever tighter. A woman of worth has learned where to place her trust and though it often takes a tougher spirit than she might want to admit, she's willing to face whatever comes knowing she is not alone.

You're a tough woman and that's a good thing. The world needs your leadership, your tenderness, and your toughness in every situation. Stay connected to your Source of strength and life, and though you may stumble, you will not fall. That is a promise!

Stay rooted in your faith!

A Worthy Thought

All our difficulties are only platforms for the manifestation of His grace, power and love.

Hudson Taylor

Lord, I don't always feel tough enough to
get through the many trials that come
my way. Please strengthen and renew
me by Your grace and power. Amen.

The Trustworthy Woman

*I love You, LORD God, and You make me strong.
You are my mighty rock, my fortress, my
protector, the rock where I am safe, my shield,
my powerful weapon, and my place of shelter.*
Psalm 18:1-2 CEV

Think of a woman in your life that you trust completely. You can tell her anything and know that it is safe to do so. You can come to her when you need support or strength of spirit. You can let your guard down with her and laugh at yourself. You feel protected by her love and sheltered in her care. Do you have someone in mind?

Now put yourself in her place. See if you are that person for her as well. One of the reasons we love someone is because we know that trust exists between us. Nothing can break the bond that keeps us safe in the relationship and we know we would do anything for each other.

You are a trustworthy woman, the strength and the fortress for someone in your life. You received an example of how to be that from God. He spreads His wings over your life and shelters you. He stands between you and anything that might make you fall. You trust Him with your life.

In friendship, trust requires that you don't always know why an event occurred or an odd situation arose. It's the same in your friendship with God. Sometimes you have to trust Him without knowing why something is as it is. Victor Hugo said, "Have courage for the great sorrows of life and patience for the small ones; and when you have laboriously accomplished your daily task, go to sleep in peace. God is awake."

A woman of worth puts her trust and her circumstances in the hand of her Supreme Protector. It is her strength and her shield.

A Worthy Thought

In God alone there is faithfulness and faith in the trust that we may hold to Him, to His promise and to His guidance. To hold to God is to rely on the fact that God is there for me, and to live in this certainty.

Karl Barth

Lord, I confess that I sometimes let the news reports and the troubles of the world come into my life and disturb my peace and disarm my trust. Help me to hold on to You, trusting You for all that happens in my life. Amen.

Becoming a
Woman of Worth

You're becoming a woman of worth every day
when you trust in God's sheltering care,
you're the teacher He sends
and the good friend who blends
sweet talk and kind thoughts meant to share.
You're becoming a woman of worth every day
with a heart that is truly God's own
for you thank Him for life
through good times and strife
and you trust that you're never alone.
You're becoming a woman of worth every day
whenever temptation comes calling,
for you know that your place
with the Savior of grace
prevents you from ever quite falling.

WORTH

The day you accepted the Son of God
into your heart and embraced
His plans for your life,
you became a woman of worth.
You've been walking that path awhile
now and you are constantly amidst
a support group of women who walk
with you, offering you a heartwarming
smile and a helping hand
whenever you need it.
Your friends in Christ are everywhere.

A Woman of Worth Is Helpful

The LORD blesses everyone who freely gives food to the poor. Arguments and fights will come to an end, if you chase away those who insult others. The king is the friend of all who are sincere and speak with kindness.
Proverbs 22:9-11 CEV

These proverbs offer guidance on how a woman of worth can be helpful to others. The first blessing comes when you help to feed the poor. Whether you literally offer your help to a soup kitchen or feed a neighbor, God sees your work and blesses you. Perhaps you find it easier to feed the spirits of those around you. If so, you'll always be needed for God will continually bring you into the same space with hungry souls.

If you stand up for others, when they are being bullied or attacked by those with mean spirits, you are a peacemaker. You help restore the balance and the possibility for good things to happen. God always blesses peacemakers for they make the world a better place for everyone.

The opposite of those who would hurl insults, is the person who speaks kindness to others. Every time you offer a kind heart and a sincere word to others, you are helping God's cause on earth. You help to bring His presence into a situation.

If you make a list today of all the ways you feel you've been helpful to people this week, see if you find these: see if you fed the heart and mind and body of anyone you know; see if you brought peace to a difficult situation and sent insulting words and ideas far away; and see if you have been a friend of the King by speaking words of sincere love and kindness to those around you. If you find those actions on your list, see if you can further your helpfulness in a new way in the days ahead. These are not things to check off a list, but things to do every day of your life.

A Worthy Thought

*Even if it's a little thing, do something for those
who have need of help, something for which
you get no pay but the privilege of doing it.*

Albert Schweitzer

Lord, I know that I can do more to help.
Open my eyes to the needs of those around
me, and move me to offer any service
I can for the sake of Jesus. Amen.

A Woman with a Humble Heart

*Humble yourselves before the
Lord, and He will lift you up.*
James 4:10

Living is a humbling experience. Whether you're on top of the game or you've fallen off the mark, you recognize that timing and circumstance and the grace of God probably played a bigger hand in where you stand, than anything you did on your own. That's humbling!

In a world that tries to make us believe that we can "have it all" or even that we can do it all, the ego stands on shaky ground. If we gave the ego full reign, it would simply send us spinning off the court because we'd exhaust ourselves in the effort to play every other person's position, as well as our own.

The ego thinks we can do everything better than anyone else can. That's a good thing for getting us in the game, but a difficult thing for keeping us there. We're always shooting for a mark we can never make.

When you overcome the needs of the ego, things begin to change. You begin to see what God designed you for, what unique role He gave you to play. He doesn't ask you to play all the positions on the court. He just asks you to play the one designed for you. Women often stretch themselves thin trying to play the best mother, wife, teacher, friend, employee, daughter, and on and on. In the end their ego suffers and they assume that they are not capable of winning the game.

Here's the secret. You have already won. You're a handpicked, first draft choice of the Coach and He has named you MVP. You're on top of the game when you accept your position with grace and humility. Stop keeping score and get out there and give life your best shot!

A Worthy Thought

We have worked, we have even worked hard;
but the question comes to us –
"What have we worked for?
Who has been our master?
With what object have we toiled?
Charles H. Spurgeon

Lord, I do work hard and I thank You for
the opportunities to do so. Keep me humble
enough to know what my job is and
what my job is not. Amen.

A Woman with a Sense of Humor

Come to my home each day and listen to me.
You will find happiness. By finding me, you
find life, and the LORD will be pleased with you.
Proverbs 8:34-35 CEV

"Someone you like is wearing an ugly hat, and she
asks you to give her your honest opinion of it:
What a lovely chapeau! But if I may make one
teensy suggestion? If it blows off, don't chase it."
Miss Piggy (from Miss Piggy's Guide to Life)

Erma Bombeck said, "I have a hat. It is graceful and feminine and gives me a certain dignity, as if I were attending a state funeral or something. Someday I may get up enough courage to wear it, instead of carrying it."

Whatever hat you wear in the world, you need to have a sense of humor. Humor is its own kind of wisdom. The voice of wisdom in today's Scripture says to come home each day and listen and you'll find happiness. Let's add to it that you need to come home each day to a sense of humor and listen to the opportunity it brings to see the joy in a situation, the laughter in the moment and the possibility that God might just want you to enjoy yourself.

Women are good at laughing at themselves regarding the fashions of the day. Designers, who drive the fashion industry don't usually stop by our houses though to ask opinions.

It's okay to lighten up and give your life the fun it was meant to have. Perhaps it is time to put your hat on, whatever its design, and have the courage to wear it for all to see. If you're smiling today, hats off to you.

A Worthy Thought

*For health and the constant enjoyment of life,
give me a keen and ever-present sense of humor;
it is the next best thing to an abiding
faith in providence.*

George B. Cheever

Lord, You have surrounded me with
many reasons to smile. Remind me that
I don't have to carry the burdens of the
world with me all the time. If I rest in
You, I can lighten up a bit. Amen.

A Woman Filled with Hope

So I pray that God, who gives you hope,
will keep you happy and full of peace as
you believe in Him. May you overflow with
hope through the power of the Holy Spirit.
Romans 15:13 NLT

Women are the divas of hope. They spend much of their lives in the pursuit of things they hope for. They pray and they hope. It may seem simple, but in truth, it's genuinely a gift from God and a blessing through the power of the Holy Spirit.

Hope means that you're not actually in control and you know it. Hope means that something is just beyond your grasp, just out of reach, harder than you thought. You hope for the good things and the right things to happen and often you hope for those things for others even more than for yourself. You hope because you can do nothing less.

Frank Laubach talked about our hope in Jesus. He said, "When compassion for the common man was born on Christmas Day, with it was born new hope among the multitudes. They feel a great, ever-rising determination to lift themselves and their children out of hunger and misery, up to a higher level. Jesus started a fire upon the earth, and it is burning hot today, the fire of a new hope in the hearts of the hungry multitudes."

Our hearts are full of hope for our own children and for all of humanity. We walk through the rain because we hope for the rainbow, God's promise to be with us. May your heart be filled with hope this week.

A Worthy Thought

*The natural flights of the human mind
are not from pleasure to pleasure,
but from hope to hope.*

Samuel Johnson

My hope rests in Your Spirit and Your love.
Help me to continue always in the blessed
hope I have in You. Amen.

An Honest Woman

*"Unless you are faithful in small matters,
you won't be faithful in large ones. If you
cheat even a little, you won't be honest
with greater responsibilities. And if you are
untrustworthy about worldly wealth, who will
trust you with the true riches of heaven?"*
Luke 16:10 11 NLT

What does it take to be an honest person all the time? Is it even possible? We can understand the idea of honesty when it comes to big things. We're able to recognize and tell the truth when it really counts. We pride ourselves in not cheating on our taxes or our spouses.

If we look far enough, and probably we don't have to look very far at all, we'll discover that we're not actually honest all the time. In fact, we may be surprised at how often we've opted to be dishonest and determined that it was okay.

If you're thinking that's not really true of you and that you would definitely call yourself an honest woman, I would say that you're right and that you are. However, I would ask you to consider things like this to gauge your own level of honesty.

When you've been asked to work late yet another night, are you able to honestly tell your employer how you feel about that? When your friend asks to borrow something from you one more time that you know will never be repaid, do you honestly express your feelings? When your spouse hasn't said, "I love you" in so long you can't remember the last time, do you honestly recognize the way that makes you feel? Sometimes honesty has nothing to do with bank balances or how we treat our neighbors. Sometimes it has to do with how honest we are with ourselves.

Walter Anderson said, "Our lives improve only when we take chances – and the first and most difficult risk we can take is to be honest with ourselves."

As a woman of worth, your intention is always to be honest. This week, try to be especially aware of those moments when you might not clearly be so.

A Worthy Thought

Honesty is the first chapter
of the book of wisdom.
Thomas Jefferson

Lord, I usually think of myself as an
honest woman. I know though that
I'm genuinely surprised if a dishonest
thought comes into my mind and even
horrified if I let it go unchecked. Help
me to be more honest with myself and
to be more honest with You. Amen.

A Woman with a Great Heart

Above all else, guard your heart,
for it affects everything you do.
Proverbs 4:23 NLT

When we think of women with a lot of heart, we usually picture those who have great sympathy for the plight of others, or those who are driven to weep for the unending tragedies of the world. Women with great hearts are usually very compassionate and considerate.

As a woman of worth, you are all of these things and God blesses your heart for all that you do. The Scripture though in one brief proverb, reminds you that it's also important to protect your heart. Why?

Antoine de Saint-Exupery said, "It is only with the heart that one can see rightly; what is essential is invisible to the eye."

Your heart is the place where God tenderly

approaches you as you walk with Him each day. He guides you to see and hear and feel those things that will increase your light and help you become an even greater friend to those around you.

When your heart sees another person, or an aspect of humanity, it moves your understanding closer to what God sees as well. When God looks at you, He sees your heart. When you look at others, you must see with the heart. It is the essential truth that helps you to love more fully.

A woman of worth is a woman with great heart for she does all she can to invest her time and talents for the good of God's other loved ones.

Protect your heart, but don't harden it. Open your heart to greater understanding of God's ways.

A Worthy Thought

The first and the great work of a Christian is about her heart. Do not be content with seeming to do good in "outward acts" while your heart is bad, and you are a stranger to the greater internal heart duties.

Jonathan Edwards

Lord, help me to open my heart
to seeing more of You in those I
meet and sharing more of You with
each new opportunity. Amen.

A Woman of Humanity

Search me, O God, and know my heart;
test me and know my thoughts.
Point out anything in me that offends You,
and lead me along the path of everlasting life.
Psalm 139:23-24 NLT

We are each connected to the other. What affects one of us, affects all of us. John Donne said, "No man is an Island, entire of itself; every man is a piece of the Continent, a part of the main."

Women understand about connection. From early on, we began forming relationships and investing in getting to know those who lived in our same spaces. We continued as we packed our little lunches and went off to school and then graduated to our homes and families, only to continue teaching our daughters the importance of love and compassion.

We're invested in our humanity and yet

we're challenged every day as we watch the news of the world to discover the enormous incongruity from one place to another. Man's inhumanity to man has never been more apparent than it is today on a global scale. As women of worth, we're called to help reestablish the balance of all that is good and humane in others.

We can start on this path by investing some time in our own prayers and our own lives. We need to understand our thoughts and how they impact others. We need to make sure we are not doing anything to offend God or His children. When we start there, we help create a new possibility for change.

We start with ourselves and then branch out to our families, our neighborhoods and the world. It is essential that we strive to have an impact for good. We cannot sit by watching humanity destroy itself and offer no opportunity to spread the light. We are called by duty, responsibility, and love to reach up and reach out to those around us. The world needs the good that only you can give.

A Worthy Thought

Only love enables humanity to grow,
because love engenders life and it is the
only form of energy that lasts forever.
Michel Quoist

Lord, the world is so overwhelming.
The need of others is so great.
Help me to do what I can wherever I am to
share my humanity in loving ways. Amen.

A Woman of Holiness

Who may climb the mountain of the LORD?
Who may stand in His holy place? Only
those whose hands and hearts are pure, who
do not worship idols and never tell lies. They
will receive the LORD's blessing and have
right standing with God their savior.
Psalm 24:3-5 NLT

There's something mysterious about the concept of being holy. It strikes an almost fearful chord that makes the heart wonder if it is even attainable. It feels like the right direction on the path, but the weeds that choke the way are without number. How do we attain pure hearts and clean hands? How do we bridge the gap between our depravity and our desire to be holy?

Mother Teresa said, "Holiness consists of doing the will of God with a smile." When the work you do for God genuinely brings you joy, you're probably on the right path. When you find yourself fussing and fuming over each thing you feel an obligation to do, you may need to reexamine your motives. Your work cannot then be holy.

Stephen Winward offered this comment about holiness, "Progress in holiness can best be measured not by the length of time we spend in prayer, not by the number of times we go to church, not by the amount of money we contribute to God's work, not by the range and depth of our knowledge of the Bible, but rather by the quality of our personal relationships."

If holiness depended on me, I'd be without recourse to move ahead. Happily, holiness depends on God who helps us understand the ways we can demonstrate holiness before Him. The quality of your personal relationships is one way to discover how well you're following Him. Let your heart be pure as you approach the work God has given you and do all things with a smile. Your holiness will come shining through.

A Worthy Thought

A true love of God must begin with a delight in His holiness, and not with a delight in any other attribute; for no other attribute is truly lovely without this.

Jonathan Edwards

Lord, sometimes I sense holiness or recognize a holy moment, but I know I don't always live in holiness. Help me to desire more of You. Amen.

A Woman Living in Harmony

Live in harmony with one another.
Romans 12:16

Finally, we've come upon something we're really good at. We know how to live in harmony. Don't we? Aren't we pretty well versed in the art of compromise and being quiet and not giving our opinion when it isn't asked for and just plain making life easier for everyone around us?

Okay, maybe that's a fantasy. Maybe we have to learn to bring harmony to a situation just like everyone else has to. Why? We need to help the world get back in tune so that we become a chorus of beauty and not a cacophony of clanging symbols. We need to help establish the order of things. It is the essential duty of love.

So how does a woman of worth seek to become something more than another noisy gong? You do so by stepping aside from the world in prayer and meditation. You learn to listen for the quiet voice inside you that guides you back to peaceful harmony for yourself. You cannot bring harmony to others if everything in your life feels like heavy metal.

Once you've reestablished your own peace, you have peace to give. Thomas à Kempis said, "What peace and inward quiet should she have who would cut away from herself all busyness of mind, and think only on heavenly things." As your thoughts take wing toward heaven's throne, sweet harmony will then be known.

Your gift this week is to find harmony in all ways ... in your family, in your work, and in your heart. God will meet you there and honor your effort to hear His voice. Be at peace with God and your life will be filled with beautiful melodies.

A Worthy Thought

Keep your heart in peace; let nothing in this world disturb it: everything has an end.

John of the Cross

Lord, as I strive for greater harmony
in my life, let me seek greater
harmony with You. Amen.

A Woman of Good Habits

If you obey all the laws and commands that I will give you today, all will be well with you and your children. Then you will enjoy a long life in the land the LORD your God is giving you for all time.
Deuteronomy 4:40 NLT

We are genuine creatures of habit. Sometimes we establish a habit without even thinking about it. We might take the same path each time we go to the grocery store or sit in the exact same pew at church or eat certain foods on our dinner plates the same way each time. Whatever it is, we appreciate routine and like to stick with it when it works well.

For some of us, that sense of routine even affects our choice of what church to attend. We grew up with a certain ritual or liturgy and now as an adult, it's what makes the church experience most fulfilling.

We even have habits in relationships. When we've gotten in the habit of treating a friend or a spouse in a certain way, we continue to do so simply out of habit. All of that can be a good thing. It can also be a thing to question.

If you say The Lord's Prayer, for example, Sunday after Sunday and don't ever pause to think about what it really means or examine whether it truly has any effect on your life that week, then the prayer itself has become more a matter of habit than of heart.

We often think habits are hard to break and typically when we say that we're thinking about bad habits. Turn that around and make your good habits hard to break. Make it nearly impossible to give up your quiet time in the morning or your dinnertime with your family. Establish the habit of always coming to the Lord with each day's plans so that you can be truly filled with each day's grace.

Look upon your habits as good things any time they further a sense of joy in your obedience to God. He's always in the habit of finding joy in you.

A Worthy Thought

We first make our habits, then
our habits make us.
John Dryden

Lord, help me to establish positive habits in
my pursuit to know more of You. Amen.

A Woman Who Understands Happiness

"Happy are those who know they are spiritually poor; the Kingdom of heaven belongs to them! Happy are those who mourn; God will comfort them! Happy are those who are humble; they will receive what God has promised! Happy are those whose greatest desire is to do what God requires; God will satisfy them fully!"
Matthew 5:3-6

Happiness depends a whole lot on what we want and what our expectations are. True happiness then is determined by how closely we align our real desires with our outcomes. The above version of Matthew 5 gives us a demonstration for happiness. It shows us some of the ways we can truly seek to be happy.

You can seek the things of God. You can be happy because you know that He'll run to meet you any time you ask. He'll not only meet you, He'll go ahead of you and beside you and behind you. In fact, you simply need to let Him know you desire to be close to Him and He'll be there. That's a great reason to be happy.

If you're sad now, you can be happy knowing that you're not alone. God is with you in your sadness and will wrap you in His love until the sadness passes and smiles reappear. If you're feeling uncertain where your home is or where you belong, you can be happy because God has plans to give you the ground on which you walk. He will be there for you every step of the way as you humbly take His hand.

If you feel the best when you're serving others, then you have every right to be happy because you'll have a continual feast. The Lord will satisfy your desire to serve in warm and loving ways and you'll never be out of a job.

A woman of worth strives to understand happiness. She doesn't count happiness like the shoes in her closet or the gemstones on her hand, but by the attitude of joy that has turned her heart totally toward God.

A Worthy Thought

Where your pleasure is, there is your treasure;
where your treasure is, there is your heart;
where your heart is, there is your happiness.

Augustine of Hippo

Lord, You have given me every reason to
be happy. Let me share that happiness
with others this week. Amen.

A Woman of Hospitality

*Keep on loving each other as brothers
and sisters. Remember to welcome strangers,
because some who have done this
have welcomed angels without knowing it.*
Hebrews 13:1-2 NCV

Most women love to entertain and enjoy the planning and the preparation that comes with having guests. We're all about being hospitable and we were taught to be so from our mothers and grandmothers.

The feeling within us that longs for a past where neighbors visited on porch swings and unexpected guests were cause for celebration, has nearly passed us by. Instead we find ourselves cocooning, protecting our homes from would-be intruders, rarely speaking to those we see in corridors of the places where we work. We don't smile at strangers because we've lost our sense of trust in each other.

We're not sure who God's people are in the world.

Today, we can still welcome others with love and open hearts within the bounds of safety and good sense. Where? You can welcome newcomers to your church. You can listen to a need, or offer comfort when you're led to do so. You can offer food for an ill neighbor or a warm coat for a homeless person. You can clean out your closets and give your still usable things to others. You can support a child in another country with the basic necessities of life. You can bake a cake for someone having a birthday in a nursing home. You can reach out to those around you.

If you do these things, will you entertain angels without knowing it? Perhaps. Will you be an angel to someone in need? Absolutely! Hospitality is always a matter of the heart. Be open to God's leading and welcome His guidance for you this week.

A Worthy Thought

*Let all guests that come be received like
Christ, for He will say, "I was a stranger
and you took Me in." Let suitable honor be
shown to all, but especially to pilgrims.*
The Rule of St. Benedict

Lord, let me offer a willing and open
heart to anyone You send my way
in the coming week. Amen.

Becoming a
Woman of Worth

You're becoming a woman of worth every day
when you honestly do your part
to give what you can to honor God's plan
of living this life with your heart.
You're becoming a woman of worth every day
when you help your neighbor to smile
giving a coat or a card that you wrote
and staying to chat for awhile.
You're becoming a woman of worth every day
when you humbly give thanks for the things
that help you to cope and constantly hope
in the happiness love always brings.